You Can Count on Me!

Joanne Mattern

Consultants

Shelley Scudder
Gifted Education Teacher
Broward County Schools

Caryn Williams, M.S.Ed.
Madison County Schools
Huntsville, AL

Publishing Credits

Conni Medina, M.A.Ed., *Managing Editor*

Lee Aucoin, *Creative Director*

Torrey Maloof, *Editor*

Marissa Rodriguez, *Designer*

Stephanie Reid, *Photo Editor*

Rachelle Cracchiolo, M.S.Ed., *Publisher*

Image Credits: Cover, p. 1 Alamy; p. 13 Corbis; p. 9 Getty Images; pp. 8, 11, 12, 14 (top), 22–23 iStockphoto; p. 4 The Library of Congress [LC-USW3-017677-E]; p. 16 The Library of Congress [LC-USZ62-136051]; p. 18 The Library of Congress [LC-DIG-ppmsca-04300]; p. 26 The Library of Congress [LC-USW3-042669-C]; p. 10 Mike Kemp/Newscom; p. 25 Peter Mason Cultura/Newscom; p. 20 REUTERS/Newscom; pp. 17, 32 Spencer T Tucker/Newscom; p. 7 The Orange County Register/Newscom; p. 21 ZUMAPRESS/Newscom; p. 6 U.S. Army; All other images Shutterstock.

Teacher Created Materials

5301 Oceanus Drive
Huntington Beach, CA 92649-1030
http://www.tcmpub.com

ISBN 978-1-4333-6995-7

© 2014 Teacher Created Materials, Inc.

Table of Contents

These kids from long ago are proud to be citizens of the United States.

What Are Citizens?

Citizens (SIT-uh-zuhns) are members of a country. Citizens in the United States have rights. They have the power to do what they want. They have freedom. But they also have responsibilities (ri-spon-suh-BIL-i-teez). These are things citizens should do.

Becoming Citizens

Kids born in the United States are citizens. Kids from other countries can become U.S. citizens, too!

These kids do not look the same but they are all U.S. citizens.

The United States is made up of many citizens. Citizens can look different and have different ideas. This is one thing that makes our country so special.

There are many things people can do to be good citizens. They can follow the rules. They can make good decisions. Good citizens can choose strong leaders. They can also help people in need.

Soldiers are good citizens. They keep our country safe.

Good citizens want to make their country a great place to live. They help keep it clean and safe. Good citizens are also proud of their country. They know its **symbols** and holidays.

These kids are picking up trash at a beach.

Rules to Live By

Every place has rules. Families have rules at home. Kids may have to clean their rooms or take out the trash. They need to listen to their parents. They have to use good manners.

This girl is cleaning her room.

Schools have rules, too. Students need to show their teachers respect. They can do this by raising their hands before speaking. Students need to be good listeners, too. They also need to be kind to their classmates. Following the rules helps keep things running smoothly.

These kids show respect by raising their hands in 1970.

There are rules for our country called *laws*. Good citizens follow the laws. One law says people should not throw trash on the ground. Good citizens put trash in trash cans. This helps keep our country clean.

This girl is picking up trash.

There are **transportation** (trans-per-TEY-shuhn) laws, too. Cars have to stop at stop signs and red lights. People have to cross the street in crosswalks. Following these laws keeps people safe.

Laws help make sure students can cross the street safely.

Stop and Think

It can be hard to follow the rules. It is not always easy to do the right thing. But our actions have **consequences** (KON-si-kwens-siz). This means that our actions affect other people.

This girl is sad because of someone else's actions.

It is a good idea to stop and think before you act. Will your actions make someone sad? Will they hurt someone? Will this choice have good or bad consequences? Thinking like this will help you make good choices.

This girl was given an award for making good choices.

People get in trouble when they make bad choices. If kids do not follow the rules at home, they may get sent to their rooms. If they do not follow the rules at school, they may get sent to the principal's office.

This girl has been sent to her room.

Sometimes adults get in trouble for breaking laws. **Punishments** (PUHN-ish-muhnts) for adults are different. They may have to pay a **fine**. Or they may even go to jail.

Grown-ups can go to jail when they break the law.

The parents are in charge in this family.

Choosing Leaders

Who is in charge in your house? The adults are probably the leaders. They make the rules. They also make sure everyone follows the rules.

This girl is giving her city's mayor a high-five.

The United States has leaders, too. A mayor is in charge of a town. A governor is in charge of a state. The president is in charge of the country. These leaders make laws that they think are fair. They make laws that keep us safe.

How does a leader get his or her job? In the United States, citizens get to choose their leaders. They **vote** in an **election** (ih-LEK-shuhn). People who want to be leaders are called **candidates** (KAN-di-deytz).

Can I Vote?

You have to be a citizen to vote. All citizens who are at least 18 years old can vote.

This woman is being a good citizen by voting.

Candidates give speeches. They tell people why they should vote for them. On Election Day, citizens can vote for the candidate they think will make the best leader. Part of being a good citizen is voting in elections.

Hillary Clinton asks people to vote for her in 2008.

These voters are celebrating their candidate's win.

Good citizens learn about the candidates before they vote. They need to know the candidates' plans for the country. This way, they can make a smart choice.

The Votes Are In!

Kids can vote for things, too. Sometimes kids get to vote for a class president or even a class pet.

This boy is voting in a school election.

People vote on laws, too. Voting is how citizens tell their leaders what they want. Voting is one of the best ways for citizens to make their voices heard. It lets them choose their leaders and their laws.

I Love My Country!

Good citizens are **patriotic** (pey-tree-OT-ik). This means they are proud of their country. There are many ways to be patriotic. You can learn about the people who made our country great. You can respect your leaders. You can help make our country a better place to live.

This boy is waving an American flag.

You can be patriotic in other ways, too. You can sing songs about our country. You can wave our country's flag.

I Pledge

Flag Day is June 14. It is the birthday of our flag. You can honor the flag by saying the Pledge of Allegiance (uh-LEE-juhns).

Good citizens know about our country's history. They know our symbols. The American flag is a symbol of our country. The stars on the flag stand for the 50 states. The bald eagle is a symbol for our country, too. It stands for our country's strength and freedom.

This is a bald eagle.

Good citizens also know about our country's holidays. The Fourth of July honors our country's freedom. Presidents' Day honors the people who have led our country.

This girl is celebrating the Fourth of July.

Be a Good Citizen

You can be a good citizen, too! You can work well with others. You can help people in need. You can follow the rules. You can speak up when you think something is wrong. You can do the right thing, even when it is hard.

These kids are helping plant a garden.

Good citizens make their country the best it can be. You do not have to be an adult to be a good citizen. What will you do to make our country better?

This boy is helping a man walk.

Sing It!

    Good citizens are patriotic. They are proud of their country. One way to be patriotic is to sing songs about your country. Learn the song on the next page and sing it to your friends. Being a good citizen can be fun!

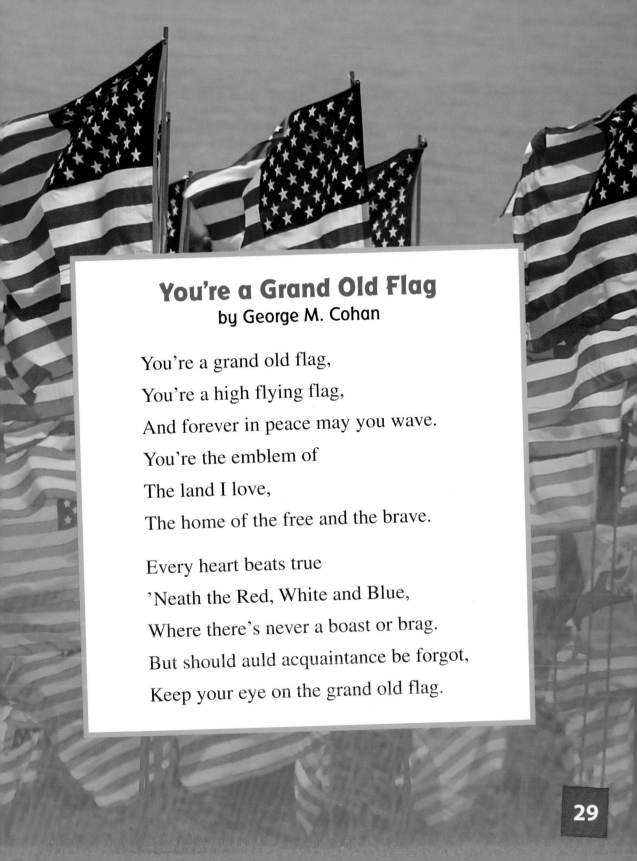

You're a Grand Old Flag
by George M. Cohan

You're a grand old flag,

You're a high flying flag,

And forever in peace may you wave.

You're the emblem of

The land I love,

The home of the free and the brave.

Every heart beats true

'Neath the Red, White and Blue,

Where there's never a boast or brag.

But should auld acquaintance be forgot,

Keep your eye on the grand old flag.

Glossary

candidates—people who want citizens to vote for them in an election

citizens—members of a country or place

consequences—the results or effects of someone's actions and choices

election—the act of voting for leaders

fine—money paid as punishment for doing something wrong

patriotic—having pride in your country

punishments—penalties for doing something wrong

symbols—things that stand for something else

transportation—cars, trucks, buses, and other moving vehicles

vote—to choose in an election

Index

Your Turn!

Lead the Way

These girls are meeting one of their city's leaders. Kids can be leaders, too. Make a list of some ways kids can be leaders. Share your list with a friend or family member.